Credit-Funded Wealth for Families

Creating Legacy Without Sacrificing Today

By Joe Correa

Published by Live Stronger Faster

This book is for educational and informational purposes only. The author and publisher are not engaged in rendering legal, financial, or other professional advice. Readers should consult a qualified professional before making any financial decisions.

First Edition

Table of Contents

Introduction

Most people believe they must choose between living a good life today or saving everything for tomorrow. It's a dilemma many families face. You want to take that vacation, fix up your home, invest in your children's future—and still build wealth that lasts for generations. But how? How do you do both when your paycheck barely stretches far enough to cover the basics?

This book was written to show you that **you don't have to choose**. You can live well today **and** build a legacy that outlives you. The key is learning how to **use credit as a tool**, not a trap. You've probably heard horror stories about families buried in debt—but what you haven't heard enough about are the families who used credit wisely and strategically to **accelerate their income**, **acquire appreciating assets**, and **secure their children's futures**. That's who this book is for.

Why This Book Matters

Credit isn't just for emergencies or short-term spending. Used correctly, it can buy you time, resources, and leverage. It can fund your first rental property. It can pay for an online business that earns passive income while you sleep. It can even help you set up life insurance policies, trusts, or college plans that are backed by real assets. **Credit, when combined with discipline and knowledge, becomes capital.**

And when capital flows through the hands of an educated family, it multiplies.

Over the past decade, I've worked with thousands of individuals, couples, and families—many of whom were immigrants or first-generation Americans—who were starting from scratch. They didn't have inherited wealth. Some had bad credit or no credit. Others had no savings. But what they did have was a willingness to learn, and a desire to build a better life for their kids.

Through trial and error, they discovered how to access tens—even hundreds—of thousands in credit, and how to convert it into income-producing vehicles like real estate, businesses, and automated side hustles. I've watched families use credit cards and lines of credit—not for shopping sprees—but for flipping properties, investing in cash flow, and creating safety nets they never had growing up.

This book is a blueprint based on their successes—and my own.

Who This Is For

If you're a parent, a caregiver, or even a single adult thinking about your financial future, this book will walk you through every step to:

- Understand and build excellent credit
- Leverage credit to invest in real assets without going into unnecessary debt
- Fund experiences for your family that create joy and memories now
- Build a strong, protective structure around your wealth so it lasts

Even if you've made financial mistakes in the past—this book is for you. Even if you've been told that credit is dangerous or you don't trust it—this book is for you. Even if you think wealth is only for "rich people"—this book will change your perspective.

Because the truth is, **families are the most powerful financial units in the world** when they work together, educate themselves, and apply the right strategies.

What to Expect

Each chapter of this book will take you through a journey—from repairing and optimizing personal credit, to learning how to access and grow business credit, to using both for long-term wealth-building. We'll explore strategies like:

- Setting up your family LLC or trust
- Buying real estate without draining your savings
- Using life insurance policies as investment vehicles
- Teaching your children about money and credit early
- Creating emergency funds, vacation funds, and investment funds—all fueled by smart credit use

You'll also hear real-world stories of families just like yours who overcame financial limitations by rethinking how they used credit. These aren't fairytales—they're practical examples with numbers, tools, and templates.

A New Financial Legacy Starts Today

You don't need to be rich to start building wealth. You just need to start.

Chapter 1: Understanding Credit as a Wealth-Building Tool

Most people think of credit as a way to *buy now and pay later*. But in reality, credit is a financial instrument—one that, when managed properly, can **accelerate your ability to earn, invest, and grow wealth**. This chapter will reframe the way you view credit and show you how to lay the foundation for building generational wealth using smart credit strategies.

The Two Types of Credit You Must Master

1. Personal Credit

Personal credit is tied to your Social Security number and tracked by the three major credit bureaus: Experian, TransUnion, and Equifax. It determines your ability to get mortgages, car loans, and personal credit cards.

Why it matters for families: A strong personal credit score can unlock:

- 0% interest promotional financing
- Higher limits on personal cards
- Low-interest HELOCs (Home Equity Lines of Credit)

- Better terms on student loans and home loans

2. Business Credit

Business credit is tied to your EIN (Employer Identification Number) and built through vendor relationships, business credit cards, and financing that doesn't report to your personal credit.

Why it matters for families: With strong business credit, you can:

- Access capital for real estate or online businesses
- Keep personal finances separate from investments
- Build a business as a family asset and legacy
- Use your LLC to write off certain expenses legally

The Wealthy Use Credit Differently

The wealthy don't fear credit—they understand it. They know that **debt tied to income-producing assets is not bad debt**. It's strategic debt. Let's compare two types of debt:

Type	Example	Result
Bad Debt	Maxing out a credit card on clothes	No ROI, long-term burden
Good Debt	Using a 0% APR card to flip a property	Asset appreciation, positive ROI

They also use credit to **free up cash**. For example:

- Use a 0% APR credit card to pay for everyday expenses, while investing your paycheck into an income-producing property.
- Get a personal line of credit to cover a down payment, then refinance after the property appreciates.

How to Use Credit Without Going Into Unmanageable Debt

Here's the key: **Credit is NOT free money—it's leveraged money.** You must treat it with the same care you would treat a business investment. Follow these principles:

1. **Only borrow with a repayment plan in place.** Never swipe unless you know how and when you'll pay it back.
2. **Use credit to buy or build assets, not liabilities.**

Ask yourself: Will this make me money or lose me money?

3. **Avoid minimum payments.** Minimums keep you in debt longer. Set up auto-pay for full balances or large payments.

4. **Keep utilization under 30%.** Even if you have $50,000 in available credit, try not to carry more than $15,000 at a time on revolving accounts.

5. **Know your numbers.** Check your FICO score regularly and monitor your credit reports for errors. Use tools like Credit Karma, Experian, or MyFICO.

Start With a Family Credit Assessment

To build credit-funded wealth, you need a full picture of where you stand.

Action Plan:

1. Pull your **credit reports** from all three bureaus at AnnualCreditReport.com.

2. List your **current debts, interest rates, and limits**.

3. Identify any **collections, missed payments, or errors**.

4. Create a 90-day goal to **increase your credit score** by:

    - Paying down debt
    - Disputing errors
    - Opening new tradelines (secured cards, retail accounts)
    - Becoming an authorized user on a family member's seasoned card

Educating Your Household

Building family wealth means involving the whole family. Teach your spouse or children (age-appropriate) the basics of credit:

- Show them how a credit card works and what interest is.
- Let them see how much you save with good credit.
- Consider adding teens as authorized users to build their credit early.

Family Credit Tip: Create a "Credit Calendar" where your household tracks:

- When payments are due
- What's being paid off
- New cards or business lines added
- Family savings goals tied to credit use

Chapter Summary:

- Credit is a powerful tool for building family wealth when used with discipline.
- The wealthy use credit to generate income and acquire assets—not to buy liabilities.
- Start with a personal and family credit audit.
- Educate every household member on the role of credit in financial freedom.

In the next chapter, we'll dive into **how to build perfect personal credit from scratch—or repair it quickly—so you can qualify for high-limit cards, lines of credit, and real estate funding.** Stay with me—this is where your wealth journey begins.

"The Breakthrough"

It was 2:17 a.m. when Miguel sat upright in bed, drenched in sweat—not from the heat, but from panic.

He had just remembered that the mortgage was due in four days, the car needed new tires, and his daughter's braces payment had bounced last week. His wife, Carla, stirred beside him. She'd been taking extra shifts at the hospital just to keep them afloat. Their son needed a laptop for school, and their youngest had outgrown all her clothes again.

They were a good family. They worked hard. They loved each other. But it never seemed to be enough.

Miguel tiptoed out of bed, grabbed a worn-out notebook from the kitchen drawer, and sat at the table. He wrote at the top of the page in capital letters: **"WHERE IS ALL THE MONEY GOING?"**

He listed every bill—mortgage, electricity, gas, groceries, insurance, credit card minimums—and even the tiny subscription charges that crept in each month unnoticed. The numbers didn't lie. They were spending more than they earned.

He looked around the modest home they had built from scratch. His eyes landed on a family photo—Carla, himself, and the three kids laughing at the beach two summers ago. He remembered how hard they'd saved for that trip. It took them eight months to put aside enough for five days of joy. And now they were slipping behind again.

Miguel whispered to himself, "There has to be a better way."

The next morning, after dropping the kids off at school, he sat in his old pickup truck and opened YouTube. He searched: "How to get out of debt and build wealth with no money." One video caught his eye—"How Families Use Credit to Build Generational Wealth." He clicked.

The speaker, a man named Joe, said something that stopped Miguel cold:

> "Credit, when used right, is not for buying things—it's for building things."

He continued:

> "The wealthy don't use credit to survive. They use it to expand—buy assets, build businesses, acquire real estate. The problem isn't credit. It's how we use it."

Miguel leaned closer. Joe broke it down further:

- Separate personal and business credit

- Fix your personal credit first
- Only use credit for things that make money, not lose it
- Leverage 0% APR credit cards, business tradelines, and HELOCs with a plan

Miguel had never heard credit explained like this before. He had always seen it as the enemy. But now... it sounded like a tool. A strategy.

He took notes. That night, he shared everything with Carla. She was skeptical at first.

> "You think we can borrow our way out of debt?" she asked.
>
> "No," Miguel replied. "I think we can *build* our way out. If we use credit not to spend, but to *invest* in something that earns income."

They started small.

First, they pulled their credit reports from AnnualCreditReport.com. There were a few errors. A couple of missed payments from years ago. An old collection that wasn't even theirs. Miguel filed disputes immediately. Then he paid off two small balances and set up autopay for all recurring bills.

Next, he applied for a secured credit card to rebuild his payment history. He added Carla as an authorized user. Within three months, their scores jumped by 72 points.

Then came the bold step: Miguel used his improved credit to apply for a 0% APR credit card with a $12,000 limit. Instead of spending it, they followed Joe's advice and used $6,000 to buy a vending machine route. Two refurbished machines, placed in busy breakrooms, generated $1,200 a month.

The payments on the card? $200/month. Profit: $1,000.

Carla couldn't believe it. "This... is working?"

Miguel smiled. "One vending machine. Imagine what we can do with five."

A year later, Miguel and Carla had used business credit to expand the vending business. They had 12 machines in total. They used a personal line of credit to pay for an online course about rental real estate and bought a small duplex using a HELOC from their improved home equity.

Every credit move they made was strategic, calculated, and backed by income.

They weren't just surviving anymore. They were saving, investing, and even taking their kids on quarterly vacations without guilt.

And every Sunday night, they held a family finance meeting where they taught their children about credit, budgeting, and investing. The kids started helping run the vending business and learning how to track expenses.

Their oldest, 16-year-old Diego, was already building his credit through a teen banking app linked to Miguel's card. Their daughter, Sofia, had started reselling vintage clothes online. The family was turning into a financial machine.

Miguel still remembered that sleepless night.

The fear. The shame. The notebook.

But now, that same notebook was filled with a wealth plan, monthly projections, and handwritten goals in bright ink: **"Buy second duplex." "Start family LLC." "Teach kids to buy their first home by 20."**

They hadn't won the lottery. They didn't get a massive raise. They simply learned how to turn credit into capital.

And that changed everything.

Chapter 2: Building Perfect Personal Credit for Long-Term Leverage

Before you can use credit to create wealth for your family, you need to start with a **solid personal credit foundation**. Whether you're starting from scratch, recovering from past mistakes, or just trying to improve your score, this chapter will walk you through the **exact steps** to build, fix, and optimize your credit profile.

Understand What Makes Up Your Credit Score

Your FICO credit score is made up of **five main components**:

Factor	Weight	What It Means
Payment History	35%	Paying on time is the most important factor
Amounts Owed (Utilization)	30%	How much credit you're using vs. your available limit
Length of Credit History	15%	The age of your oldest and newest accounts

Credit Mix	10%	Types of credit (loans, cards, mortgage, etc.)
New Credit	10%	Recent inquiries and newly opened accounts

To build strong credit, focus first on **paying everything on time**, then **keep your balances low**—ideally under 30% of each card's limit.

Repair Your Credit File if Needed

If your credit has collections, charge-offs, or late payments, **don't ignore them. Fix them.**

Action Steps:

1. **Get Your Free Reports** Visit AnnualCreditReport.com to download all three bureau reports.
2. **Identify Errors and Negative Items** Look for:
    - Incorrect names or addresses
    - Accounts you don't recognize
    - Late payments you're sure were paid on time
    - Collections that should have aged off (7+ years)

3. **Dispute Inaccuracies** File online or via certified mail with supporting evidence. Each bureau must respond within 30 days.

4. **Negotiate Pay-for-Delete Deals** Some collectors will remove the negative item if you pay in full or settle the balance.

5. **Use the Goodwill Letter Strategy** If you have a solid history with a creditor, request that they remove a late payment out of goodwill.

Add Positive Tradelines to Boost Your Score

If you're lacking positive accounts, **you'll need to build new ones**. Here's how:

Credit-Building Tools:

- **Secured Credit Cards**: You deposit $200–$500 as collateral and build history with responsible use.

- **Retail Store Cards**: Easier to get approved for, even with average credit.

- **Authorized User Accounts**: Ask a family member with great credit to add you to one of their cards. Their history will reflect on your report.

- **Credit Builder Loans**: You "pay yourself" into a locked savings account while building payment history.
- **Rental Reporting Services**: Report on-time rent payments to bureaus through services like RentReporters or Experian Boost.

Use Credit Without Hurting Your Score

Here are the rules to **build and maintain high credit scores**:

- **Pay ON TIME—every time.** Even one 30-day late payment can drop your score 80+ points.
- **Keep utilization under 30% on each card.** Under 10% is ideal.
- **Don't close old accounts.** Length of history matters.
- **Only apply for new credit when you need it.** Too many inquiries can hurt your score short-term.
- **Set auto-pay on at least the minimum due.** Prevents late payments automatically.

Achieve a 700+ Score in 90–180 Days

With consistency, even someone recovering from bad credit

can reach a strong credit score in just a few months.

Sample 90-Day Plan:

1. **Month 1**
    - Pull reports and dispute any errors
    - Get a secured credit card
    - Pay off past-due accounts
2. **Month 2**
    - Become an authorized user on a seasoned account
    - Use your card for small purchases and pay in full
    - Report rent and utility payments
3. **Month 3**
    - Apply for a retail card to diversify mix
    - Keep utilization under 10%
    - Track your score weekly (use Credit Karma or MyFICO)

By the end of this process, you'll be in a **position to qualify** for:

- High-limit credit cards
- Low-interest personal lines
- Mortgage pre-approvals
- Auto loans with no money down

Chapter Summary:

- Building personal credit is the **first major step** toward family wealth creation.
- Focus on **payment history** and **credit utilization** above all else.
- Use **positive tradelines** like secured cards and rental history to boost your file.
- A clean, high-scoring personal credit profile unlocks low-cost capital.

"Fixing Credit, Rebuilding Life"

April stood in the checkout line at Target, holding her breath as the cashier swiped her card.

Declined.

The cashier glanced up with an apologetic smile. April's heart sank. Her 9-year-old daughter, Ava, stood beside her, clutching a box of crayons and a pink backpack they had picked out for the first day of school.

April forced a calm voice. "Let me try another one."

Her second card worked—barely. The receipt showed she had less than $7 left in her account.

That night, after tucking Ava into bed, April sat in the kitchen with her laptop, a notepad, and a heavy heart. She hadn't always struggled this way. Five years earlier, she had a decent job, decent credit, and a small savings account. But then came the divorce, the medical bills, the missed payments, and the endless juggling of cards to stay afloat.

She was tired of living this way—tired of the anxiety, the late fees, the phone calls from creditors. And most of all, tired of telling Ava "not this time" when she asked for little things other kids seemed to take for granted.

April Googled "how to fix bad credit" and stumbled onto a podcast episode titled **"How a Single Mom Went from 480 to 780 Credit Score and Bought Her First Home."**

She clicked play.

The guest talked about pulling credit reports, finding errors, sending dispute letters, building new tradelines—even using rent and utility payments to boost her score. It all sounded... doable.

April grabbed her notepad and started writing a plan.

Step 1: Pull All Three Credit Reports

She visited AnnualCreditReport.com and downloaded her reports from Experian, Equifax, and TransUnion.

She stared at the pages, overwhelmed at first—but determined.

She saw a store card she never opened, a collection for a cable bill she didn't owe, and several late payments from a joint account her ex had stopped paying without telling her.

She circled them all.

Step 2: Dispute and Clean Up

April learned how to file disputes online and by certified mail. She created a simple spreadsheet to track each dispute, the bureau, the reason, and the response date.

A month later, **two accounts were removed** and one had the late payment updated to "paid on time." Her score jumped 46 points in just four weeks.

Step 3: Add Positive Credit

April applied for a **secured credit card** with a $300 deposit. She used it only for gas and groceries and paid it off every Friday.

She also signed up for **Experian Boost** to add her rent and utility payments to her credit report. Within two months, she had three new positive tradelines reporting.

Encouraged, she asked her older sister to add her as an **authorized user** on a long-standing credit card with a $10,000 limit and perfect history. Within a week, her score jumped another 32 points.

Step 4: Keep Building

By month four, April was approved for a retail store card and another unsecured credit card with a $1,000 limit. She kept utilization under 10%, never missed a payment, and watched her credit score cross 700 for the first time in her adult life.

With her improved credit, she applied for a **low-interest personal loan** to consolidate her remaining debts. Her monthly payments dropped by $120, and she paid off two high-interest cards.

Step 5: Family Goals

Ava noticed the difference. No more declined cards. Groceries paid on time.

A Saturday morning trip to the farmer's market where April let her pick out fresh fruit and flowers.

"Mommy, we rich now?" Ava asked with a big grin.

April laughed. "Not yet, sweetie. But we're getting smarter with our money."

They started a ritual: every Sunday, they sat together and wrote out their goals.

Ava's: "Get a dog." April's: "Buy a home."

12 Months Later...

April had done it. Her score was 756. She had three revolving accounts, two installment accounts, zero late payments, and a growing emergency fund.

She was pre-approved for a mortgage.

More importantly, she was confident. In control. And finally free from the shadow of bad credit.

She had turned a nightmare into a blueprint.

One step at a time.

And now she was helping other single moms do the same.

“Credit,” she said at her local workshop, “is not a trap if you learn how to use it. It’s a key. A key to everything you were told you couldn’t have.”

Chapter 3: Building Business Credit as a Family Asset

Most families focus only on personal credit–missing out on one of the **most powerful wealth tools available**: **business credit**. It doesn't rely on your Social Security number, doesn't impact your personal credit scores when used wisely, and can be scaled far beyond typical personal credit limits. In this chapter, you'll learn how to **establish, grow, and leverage business credit** to fund your family's long-term financial goals.

Why Business Credit Matters for Families

Business credit allows you to:

- Access higher limits with fewer personal guarantees
- Fund real estate, online businesses, and side hustles
- Protect your personal credit from overuse
- Turn your family into an income-producing "business unit"
- Pass down a real, cash-generating business to your children

Most importantly, **business credit is scalable**. A well-structured business can receive $50,000–$250,000 in credit within 12–18 months—even faster with the right strategies.

Set Up a Real, Fundable Business

Before applying for business credit, your company must look legitimate and meet lender standards—this is called being **"fundable"**.

Action Steps:

1. **Choose a Business Structure**
    - Register an **LLC** or **Corporation** (avoid sole proprietorships)
    - Use a state website or filing service to register
2. **Get an EIN**
    - Apply for free at the IRS website
3. **Open a Business Bank Account**
    - Use your EIN and formation documents to open an account
    - Deposit $100–$500 to get started

4. **Get a Professional Business Address & Phone Number**

    - Don't use a P.O. box or home address if avoidable
    - Set up a virtual address (ex: iPostal1, Regus)
    - Get a business phone number (Google Voice, RingCentral)

5. **List Your Business Online**

    - Register with 411 directory
    - Build a basic website and get a business email (yourname@yourcompany.com)

Lenders and vendors will research you. If your business looks unprofessional or incomplete, you won't get approved.

Start Building Vendor Credit (Net-30 Accounts)

Vendor credit, or **Net-30 accounts**, report to business credit bureaus and help you **build your business credit file from scratch**.

Start with 3–5 vendors that report:

Vendor	What They Offer	Reports To
Uline	Office and shipping supplies	D&B, Experian
Grainger	Industrial products	D&B, Equifax
Quill	Office and cleaning supplies	D&B
Crown Office Supplies	School & office items	Equifax, CreditSafe
NAV	Credit monitoring & reports	D&B, Experian

How to Use Them:

- Order $50–$100 of products you already need
- Pay the invoice early or on time
- Repeat monthly for 2–3 months

After 3–5 vendors report, you'll generate your **Paydex Score** (Dun & Bradstreet's version of a credit score).

Move to Tier 2 – Retail Business Credit Cards

Once your business has a few tradelines reporting, apply for

store credit cards in your business's name. These do not require personal guarantees if your credit file is strong.

Examples:

- Amazon Business
- Lowe's Pro Business
- Shell, BP, or Chevron gas cards
- Dell Business Credit

Again, **only use what you can pay off monthly.** This is to grow your credit limits and build history—not to spend unnecessarily.

Graduate to Tier 3 – High-Limit Business Credit Cards and Loans

After 6–9 months of on-time payments with vendors and retail accounts, you'll be positioned to apply for:

- **Business credit cards** (Amex Blue Business Plus, Capital One Spark, Chase Ink)
- **Business lines of credit** ($10K–$100K)
- **Equipment financing, vehicle loans, and SBA funding**

You may still be asked for a **personal guarantee**, especially early on. But over time, as your business credit deepens, you'll access funding **with no PG**.

Pro Tip: Apply with **banks that you already have business accounts with**, as they're more likely to approve you.

Chapter Summary:

- Business credit can fuel your family's long-term wealth goals and protect your personal finances.
- Set up a **fundable business** with a legal structure, EIN, address, phone, website, and bank account.
- Start with **vendor accounts** to build your profile, then move up to **retail and high-limit credit**.
- Use business credit to fund **income-generating ventures**, not liabilities.

"The Family Business That Credit Built"

Victor Martinez stood in his garage, looking at a pile of used power tools stacked beside a half-built workbench. His 15-year-old son, Leo, was scrolling through his phone on the tailgate of Victor's dusty truck, bored.

"Dad," Leo said without looking up, "why don't you just sell them?"

Victor turned. "What, the tools?"

"Yeah. You've got, like, ten drills and four sanders. Sell 'em online."

Victor laughed. "People don't buy used tools like they used to."

Leo tapped his screen. "Actually... they do."

That conversation, as small and casual as it seemed, would change their family's life forever.

That night, Victor talked to his wife, Angela, over dinner. He'd been laid off from his warehouse job three months earlier. Angela was covering them with her nursing shifts, but they both knew they needed another source of income. Leo's comment stuck with him.

"What if we started a little tool resale business?" he asked. Angela raised an eyebrow. "With what money?"

Victor shrugged. "Maybe we could use some of our credit... but smart this time."

Angela was hesitant. Years ago, they had gotten into trouble with credit cards. But Victor had been reading about **business**

credit—credit that wouldn't be tied to their personal names.

The Setup

Victor filed for an LLC that weekend—**"Tool Time Traders LLC."** He got an EIN for free on the IRS website and opened a business checking account with $250 from their tax return.

He registered a virtual business address and bought a simple domain name: *ToolTimeTraders.com.*

Then, he applied for Net-30 accounts with Uline, Quill, and Grainger. He ordered $60 worth of cleaning supplies and shipping tape, paid the invoices early, and watched his business credit profile come to life.

Every week, Victor taught Leo how to list items on Facebook Marketplace, eBay, and OfferUp. They posted pictures, wrote descriptions, and even learned how to bundle tools for higher profit margins. In just one month, they made over $1,000.

Angela noticed something different. They weren't just selling things—they were **working together as a family**.

The Climb

By month three, Victor had four vendors reporting on his business credit profile. His Paydex score showed up on Dun & Bradstreet.

He applied for an Amazon Business credit line and got approved for $4,000.

He bought a used lot of returned tools from a supplier in Georgia—paid with the Amazon Business account—and resold it locally for a 45% profit.

Then came the big milestone: approval for the **Chase Ink Business Cash** card with a $10,000 limit.

Angela was shocked. "Isn't that too much risk?"

Victor shook his head. "We're not using it to buy clothes or go on vacation. This card only touches things that make us money."

The Transformation

Within a year, Tool Time Traders was earning $4,000–$6,000 a month. Victor and Leo rented a small warehouse space with a delivery bay. Leo learned how to create simple video ads on TikTok, showing their "tool hauls," and built a following of 12,000 people.

Angela eventually cut back on her night shifts. She started managing the books and found more suppliers to negotiate with.

They added a service division—local tool repair and sharpening, run by a family friend who needed work. They even started teaching other families how to start their own credit-backed side businesses.

The Legacy

What started with a casual conversation turned into a **fully functional family business**, built on smart credit and fueled by unity.

Leo, now a high school junior, had a 760 credit score as an authorized user on one of the company's oldest cards. He planned to launch his own ecommerce store and major in business finance.

Victor had a vision board in his office. On it, three goals:

1. Buy a commercial property with business credit.
2. Fund Leo's college education without student loans.
3. Teach 100 other families how to do the same.

"I used to think credit was a trap," he said at a local seminar. "But now I know—it's a ladder. You just have to climb it the right way."

Chapter 4: Using Credit to Acquire Real Estate Without Draining Savings

For many families, owning real estate is the ultimate wealth-building goal. But with high prices, down payments, and closing costs, the dream can feel out of reach. The truth is, you can start acquiring properties using **credit strategically**—without draining your family's savings.

In this chapter, you'll learn exactly how to use personal and business credit to **fund down payments, cover rehab costs, and cash flow real estate**—all while protecting your financial foundation.

Why Real Estate Is Ideal for Credit-Backed Wealth

Real estate is one of the best investments to leverage credit because:

- It's a tangible, appreciating asset
- It produces monthly cash flow through rent
- It can be improved to increase value
- It offers tax deductions (mortgage interest, depreciation, etc.)

- Lenders allow **leverage**—you don't need to pay full price

Credit, when used correctly, can cover:

- Down payments
- Closing costs
- Renovations
- Furnishing for short-term rentals
- Bridge financing until long-term financing is secured

Funding Down Payments Using Credit

Important: Mortgage lenders typically don't allow **borrowed money** for down payments—unless it's from a **secured** source like a HELOC or business line of credit.

Strategies:

1. **Home Equity Line of Credit (HELOC)**
    - If you already own a home, use your equity to fund another property.
    - A $100K HELOC at 7% interest costs roughly $583/month interest-only.

- Use HELOC to fund a down payment, then refinance or pay off quickly.

2. **Business Credit Card with 0% APR**
    - Use a 0% card to fund closing costs or small rehab projects.
    - Many business cards offer 12–18 months of no interest.

3. **Personal Line of Credit**
    - These can be used for down payments if you repay quickly.
    - Some banks offer $10K–$50K unsecured lines at competitive rates.

4. **Cash Advance to Purchase Options Contract**
    - Use credit to pay for a real estate option or earnest deposit.
    - Flip the contract (wholesale) or assign it to another investor.

Financing Property Repairs and Improvements with Credit

Real estate investors often fund renovations with **credit**

cards, **business lines of credit**, or **vendor credit**.

Example:

- You purchase a fixer-upper for $180,000 with a 20% down payment ($36,000).
- You use a $15,000 business credit card at 0% APR to renovate.
- After repairs, the property appraises for $250,000.
- You refinance at the new value, pay off the card, and pull out equity.

This method is commonly known as the **BRRRR Method**: **Buy – Rehab – Rent – Refinance – Repeat.**

Create a Real Estate Investment Entity

To protect your personal assets and grow business credit:

1. Create an **LLC** specifically for real estate investing.
2. Use your LLC to:
    - Open business bank accounts
    - Apply for lines of credit and credit cards

- Purchase insurance and services
- Hold rental properties

3. Keep detailed records of income, expenses, and debt payments.

Having a formal business structure makes it easier to get funding, partner with investors, and pass properties on to heirs.

Risk Management and Smart Exit Planning

Credit can accelerate your wealth—but misused, it can create financial strain.

Tips to stay safe:

- **Use interest-free periods wisely.** Always have an exit strategy.
- **Avoid long-term balances on high-interest cards.**
- **Build multiple streams of income** from the property: long-term rental, Airbnb, storage space, etc.
- **Always have a reserve fund** for emergencies or vacancies.

- **Set up asset protection**: trusts, insurance, LLC layers.

If your plan is to flip the property, **have contractors, timelines, and resale strategies in place before swiping a card.**

If your plan is to hold and rent, **run cash flow numbers carefully**, including mortgage, taxes, insurance, utilities, and credit payments.

Chapter Summary:

- You can use credit to start building your real estate portfolio—without wiping out your savings.
- Use HELOCs, business cards, and lines of credit for down payments, repairs, and scaling.
- Create a real estate investment LLC to protect yourself and qualify for more funding.
- Always plan your exit, your refinance, or your repayment strategy in advance.

"From One Flip to Freedom"

The Thomas family didn't look like real estate investors.

Monica worked full-time as a 4th-grade teacher. Her husband, Darren, was a school bus mechanic who picked up extra shifts fixing cars on weekends. Their two daughters, Jade and Laila, were used to tagging along on trips to the hardware store—not for home projects, but because their parents were always fixing something for someone else.

The family had dreams—big ones. They wanted a second income. Monica had always wanted to travel. Darren dreamed of owning land. But with only a few thousand in savings and two maxed-out credit cards, those dreams seemed far off.

Until one day, while scrolling through YouTube videos about saving for retirement, Monica stumbled on a video titled: **"How I Flipped a House with Business Credit and Made $47K in 90 Days."**

She played the video on the TV.

Darren, half-listening while organizing his tools, perked up when the speaker said,

> "You don't need cash—you need credit and a plan."

That night, they stayed up talking.

Monica said, "What if we use our tax refund to start an LLC and get a business credit card?"

Darren raised an eyebrow. "To buy a house?"

"No," she said. "To flip a house. Or at least fix it up. Just one. If it works, we try again."

Getting Started

With $1,800 from their refund, Monica formed **T&L Property Solutions LLC**—named after their daughters, Thomas and Laila. She opened a business bank account, got a virtual address, and signed up for a business credit builder program online.

Within 60 days, they had:

- A business credit profile
- 4 vendor accounts reporting
- An 80 Paydex score with Dun & Bradstreet
- A $12,000 business credit card with 0% APR for 12 months

Then came the chance they were waiting for.

Darren's cousin, who had inherited a run-down home just outside Tampa, offered to sell it to them for $147,000—$30K under market value.

The catch? It needed repairs. Fast.

The Flip

The Thomases used $25,000 from the business card for:

- Roofing repairs
- Kitchen cabinets
- Paint, fixtures, and landscaping
- A handyman for plumbing work

Darren did the rest himself, using weekends and evenings to get the home ready for resale.

They kept every receipt, tracked every expense, and took photos of every improvement.

Monica handled the listings. Within three weeks of completion, they had three offers. They accepted one for **$219,000**.

Their profit after closing costs and fees? **$39,200.**

They paid off the business credit card. In full.

The Pivot

But something changed after the flip.

Instead of cashing out and spending the profits, they sat down at the kitchen table and asked themselves: **"What if we did this again? But this time... what if we held onto the property?"**

They started looking into BRRRR: Buy, Rehab, Rent, Refinance, Repeat.

Using $10,000 of their profit, they found a small duplex in an up-and-coming area. They bought it using a hard money loan for purchase, then used their **business card again for repairs.**

After it was rented and refinanced, the cash-out allowed them to repay all debts and clear $450/month in cash flow.

The Family Shift

Jade, now 12, started helping Darren calculate renovation costs and watching Zillow to find "ugly houses" that could be next.

Laila asked if she could design the next Airbnb listing's room "so it looks cooler."

Monica created a Sunday ritual—real estate finance lessons around the dinner table. "How much did we spend?" "What's the rent?" "What's our monthly profit?"

Darren started teaching younger mechanics about how he used credit to fund tools, fix homes, and reinvest.

They weren't just flipping houses. They were **flipping their mindset**—from paycheck-to-paycheck to strategic, generational wealth.

One Year Later

T&L Property Solutions had:

- Completed 2 flips
- Held 3 rental units
- Received approval for a $50,000 line of credit from their local bank
- Created a family mission statement: "We don't borrow to survive. We borrow to grow."

They still lived modestly.

Still worked.

But now they had options.

And that was worth more than any raise they'd ever been promised.

Chapter 5: Creating Multiple Income Streams Using Credit

Relying on one paycheck is a risky strategy in today's economy. Families that build real wealth often do so by developing **multiple streams of income**—and many of them start by leveraging **credit** to launch, fund, or scale these income streams.

In this chapter, you'll learn how to use personal and business credit to **create diversified, family-friendly income sources** that can be managed part-time but produce long-term results.

Why Multiple Streams of Income Matter

Depending on one job or source of income makes your financial foundation fragile. But adding even **one or two supplemental income streams** can:

- Make you recession-resistant
- Provide security during emergencies
- Fund future investments
- Help pay off debt faster

- Create long-term family stability

Most wealthy families have 4 to 7 income streams, including:

- Rental income
- Online business income
- Dividend/interest income
- Royalties
- Freelance or consulting income
- Product sales
- Passive investments

Credit is the engine that can power the startup of these streams when cash is limited.

Credit-Backed Income Stream Ideas for Families

Here are proven income streams that can be launched or scaled using personal or business credit:

1. Ecommerce Business (Amazon, eBay, Shopify)

- Use credit to buy inventory, website setup, and product packaging.

- Business cards help fund order fulfillment and ad campaigns.
- ROI potential: 15–40% profit margin.

2. Short-Term Rentals (Airbnb)

- Use credit to furnish a rental, stage a home, or pay for digital marketing.
- Set up an LLC to manage the property.
- Use business credit for cleaning equipment, welcome kits, and insurance.

3. Online Course or Coaching Business

- Credit can cover course creation software, video tools, ads, and branding.
- Passive income potential once the product is complete.

4. Vending Machine or ATM Business

- Use business cards for initial machine purchase and placement fees.
- Ongoing cash flow once established.

5. Turo (Car Sharing) or Toro (Tool Sharing)

- Use credit to buy or lease a vehicle or high-value tools to rent.
- Market locally or through platforms.
- Write off expenses as business deductions.

Smart Use of Credit to Launch Your Income Stream

When launching an income stream with credit, follow these principles:

Do:

- Use **0% interest cards** for startup expenses.
- Have a **repayment plan** tied to projected income.
- Track **every dollar** you spend and earn.
- Open a **separate account** for the business side hustle.
- Limit use to **revenue-generating activities**.

Don't:

- Max out credit limits.
- Spend before validating your business model.
- Mix personal and business transactions.

- Use credit to fund lifestyle upgrades.

Example: If you use a $5,000 0% card to launch an online course, and it generates $1,500/month, you can pay off the balance in 4 months—leaving 8 months of pure profit before interest kicks in.

Involve the Family in the Income Stream

Turning your side income into a **family project** creates shared purpose and teaches financial skills early. Depending on age and interest, your children and spouse can help with:

- Product research
- Video editing
- Managing social media
- Shipping and packaging
- Bookkeeping
- Customer service

This builds financial literacy and generational wealth habits at home.

Scale and Stack Income Streams Over Time

Once you launch one income stream and it's stable, reinvest profits or reuse available credit to build **a second one**. This could look like:

1. Start with ecommerce using business credit
2. Use profits to fund a real estate down payment
3. Use rental income to support online course creation
4. Layer in passive income with affiliate marketing or royalty-based content

You'll move from **active effort** to **automated income** over time—freeing up hours and reducing financial pressure.

Chapter Summary:

- One income is risky. Smart families use credit to build **multiple income streams**.
- Start small with ecommerce, content creation, or vending—anything that can cash flow quickly.
- Always use **credit tied to revenue**, not spending.
- Involve your family and reinvest profits to stack streams.

"Weekends into Wealth"

The Reeds weren't rich. They weren't influencers. They weren't investors or trust fund kids. But they were **builders**—and not the kind that worked in construction.

Chris was a middle school science teacher. His wife, Yasmine, worked at the public library. Their three boys—Miles (13), Kian (10), and Noah (7)—kept them busy with soccer games, messy backpacks, and endless grocery runs. Most weekends, the Reeds just tried to survive.

But one Friday night, as they sat around the table reviewing bills and deciding whether to delay a car repair, Yasmine blurted out, "We have to stop depending on just these two checks."

Chris nodded, exhausted. "I know. But we don't exactly have a pile of cash to start something."

Yasmine grabbed her phone and pulled up a note labeled: **"Family Income Streams – Start with Credit."**

They had watched a webinar the week before about using **business credit to launch side hustles**. The speaker broke it down clearly:

"You don't need capital. You need credit and a plan."

Yasmine had written down three ideas. They decided to start all of them—with credit.

Income Stream #1: Vending Machine Side Hustle

Using a $6,000 **business credit card with 0% APR for 12 months**, Chris bought two used vending machines and stocked them with snacks from Costco. He placed them in the breakroom of a local auto repair chain—after pitching the owner on a "no-maintenance, revenue-share" deal.

By month two, the machines were pulling in $600/month. After restocking costs and a small cut to the shop, they netted $350/month.

Chris had the boys help stock the machines on Saturday mornings. Kian handled the coins. Noah cleaned the glass. Miles tracked the sales on a spreadsheet.

It became a family ritual—and a business lesson rolled into one.

Income Stream #2: Digital Products Business

Yasmine had always created fun educational worksheets for her library's after-school program. Using a Canva Pro subscription (paid via a $120 business credit), she turned those worksheets into **downloadable activity bundles** for teachers and homeschoolers.

She listed them on Etsy and TeachersPayTeachers.

The initial $500 she spent on templates, branding, and a short Fiverr gig paid off in six weeks. Her bundles were earning $40–$60 a day in sales.

The boys helped name the bundles and even suggested themes: "Space Math," "Zombie Grammar," and "Fortnite Vocab."

By month four, she had created over 40 digital products—each one taking just 1–2 hours to build.

Income Stream #3: Car Rental (Turo)

Chris had recently paid off their second car. Rather than sell it, he listed it on **Turo**, a car-sharing platform. They used **business credit to purchase insurance, detailing, and a key safe** for self-check-in.

They rented it out on weekends and during school breaks—pulling in $400–$600 per month.

Chris and Miles made it a project—tracking mileage, cleaning, and handling customer hand-offs. It gave Miles real-world business exposure and something to be proud of.

One Year Later

The Reeds were earning **an extra $2,500/month** from their three side hustles.

- The vending machines grew to 5 units across 3 locations
- Yasmine's digital shop passed $20,000 in sales
- Their Turo car paid for itself and was upgraded with a newer, more fuel-efficient model—also credit-funded

They had **paid off all original credit balances** used to launch the projects. Their credit scores improved. They were pre-approved for a line of credit from their bank. And they started looking into a small Airbnb investment using the same principles they'd applied all year.

But the best part?

Their kids now knew what a "profit margin" was. They knew how to write a pitch email. And they understood the difference between **using credit to survive** and **using credit to grow.**

One Sunday morning, Noah asked, “Can we start a YouTube channel to show other families how to make money too?”

Yasmine smiled. “That’s a fourth stream of income, baby.”

Chapter 6: Protecting and Preserving Family Wealth with Credit-Funded Tools

Creating wealth is only half the equation. The other half is **protecting what you've built**. Without a plan, wealth can disappear as fast as it's created—from emergencies, lawsuits, economic downturns, or poor planning. This chapter focuses on using **credit-funded resources** to establish **legal, financial, and protective systems** that keep your family's income and assets safe for the long term.

Why Protection Matters

Here's the reality:

- 70% of families lose their wealth by the second generation.
- 90% lose it by the third.
- Most families don't lose it from bad decisions—they lose it from **no decisions**.

By using **credit strategically**, you can afford the tools and structures that preserve your legacy **now**, rather than waiting until you're "rich enough."

Credit-Funded Wealth Protection Tools

Let's explore the tools that help protect your income, property, and future—and how you can **fund them with credit** if necessary:

1. Insurance (Life, Property, and Liability)

- Life insurance protects your family if something happens to you.
- Umbrella policies protect you from lawsuits.
- Landlord or business insurance protects real estate and income streams.

Use 0% APR credit cards or business credit lines to prepay annual premiums at a discount.

2. LLCs and Legal Entities

- LLCs separate your personal assets from your business or rental properties.
- If you're sued, only the LLC's assets are at risk—not your family's home or savings.
- Series LLCs allow you to protect multiple assets under one structure.

Startup costs for LLCs ($150–$500) can be covered with business credit or reimbursement from side income.

3. Revocable Living Trusts

- Avoid probate, protect privacy, and ensure your wealth is passed on as you choose.
- You can name successors, guardians for children, and stipulate how wealth is distributed.

If legal fees are a barrier ($500–$2,000), fund it through a legal credit line or legal financing program.

4. Asset-Building Life Insurance (IUL or Whole Life)

- These policies **build cash value**, which you can **borrow against tax-free**.
- The policy protects your family and becomes a **credit-like wealth tool** over time.

Use a short-term credit strategy to afford early premiums while you build equity.

5. Emergency Funds and Credit Access

- Build a reserve for unexpected expenses using a **business credit card or line of credit**, only when needed.
- Keep personal credit intact for major life changes or backup funding.

Establish a credit-backed "family emergency account" as a line you don't use unless it's absolutely necessary.

Teach the Family to Protect What You've Built

Wealth is more easily protected when the whole family understands what's at stake and how to manage it.

Build a Family Wealth Protection Plan:

- Set up a monthly family financial review (even with young children).
- Share age-appropriate lessons about credit, risk, and responsibility.
- Document logins, passwords, asset accounts, and contacts in a secured file.
- Record a simple family video legacy explaining your financial decisions and values.

> "Wealth without education disappears. But wealth with wisdom becomes legacy."

Affordable Protection Strategies Using Credit

Sometimes you're ready to build protection—but cash is tight. These options help bridge the gap:

Protection Tool	**Average Cost**	**How to Use Credit**
Life Insurance	$30–$200/month	Use 0% card for first year premiums
LLC Formation	$150–$500	Use business card or legal credit service
Estate Plan or Trust	$500–$2,000	Finance via legal firms or personal line
Emergency Fund Setup	$1,000–$5,000	Use business line or personal loan to establish backup
Legal Shield/Identity Theft	$30–$80/month	Use card with cashback or auto-pay setup

Start small if needed. Even **partial protection is better than none.**

Your Family Legacy Blueprint

By this point, you've already started creating wealth. Now it's time to **write your family legacy playbook**.

Include:

- Your values and vision
- What you want to pass on (assets, businesses, education)
- Instructions for property, passwords, and responsibilities
- How future generations should handle credit and debt
- A plan for each child to build credit early and avoid mistakes

This blueprint becomes a **living family financial manual**—one that can be printed, recorded, and passed on.

Chapter Summary:

- Protecting wealth is just as important as creating it.

- Use credit strategically to fund insurance, legal entities, and emergency resources.
- Teach your family how to preserve and expand what you've built.
- Create a formal plan that outlives you—and empowers your children.

"Guardians of the Legacy"

Camila adjusted the folders on her lap as the notary slid a packet of estate planning documents across the table. Her husband, Elijah, sat next to her, still in his work boots, a little out of place in the polished law office. Their kids—Ari (16) and Micah (13)—waited in the car, listening to music and texting friends.

Neither Camila nor Elijah had grown up with wealth. Elijah's father worked the fields in Central Florida. Camila's mother cleaned houses. They had learned to survive, not build.

But that was changing.

Ten years ago, they'd started a small mobile detailing business—Elijah cleaning cars while Camila handled marketing and scheduling. Over time, they added services, hired help, and eventually turned it into a thriving operation that brought in more money than their old 9-to-5s combined.

They used **business credit** to scale. They used **personal credit** to buy their first duplex. They used both to fund a real estate portfolio of four rentals and one Airbnb.

And now, they were doing something that no one in their family history had ever done: **Protecting it.**

A Wake-Up Call

Two months earlier, Elijah's childhood friend Rico had passed away unexpectedly at 39. No will. No trust. No insurance.

His wife was left scrambling to handle funeral costs, creditors, and three kids—without access to Rico's bank accounts, without knowledge of his business finances, and without any legal rights to his property.

It hit Elijah like a punch to the gut.

"We're building all this for the kids," he told Camila that night. "But what happens if I don't wake up tomorrow?"

Camila squeezed his hand. "We fix it. Now."

The Legacy Plan Begins

They started with life insurance.

Using a **business credit card with 0% APR**, they prepaid for both of their term policies for the first year—saving $200 by paying annually instead of monthly. The peace of mind was immediate.

Next, they booked a free consultation with a family attorney. The attorney suggested a **revocable living trust** to avoid probate, a **healthcare directive**, a **will**, and setting up each property in **separate LLCs** for asset protection.

The legal costs were $2,100.

Camila opened a **personal line of credit** they had been approved for months ago but never used. She used $2,000 from it to pay the legal retainer—then set up a six-month repayment plan from their Airbnb income.

"Why wait until we 'have the money,'" she said, "when we have **access** to money and a plan to pay it back?"

Bringing the Kids In

One Sunday, they sat Ari and Micah down and told them everything.

They explained:

- What a trust was
- Why they had life insurance
- What happens if something happened to Mom or Dad
- Why they weren't just leaving money—they were leaving a **map**

Ari, skeptical but intrigued, asked, "So... you guys are planning for when you're not here?"

"We're planning so you never have to scramble like we did," Camila said.

That afternoon, they drafted a simple **Family Wealth Legacy Book**—a binder with:

- Passwords
- Bank accounts
- Deeds and LLC documents
- Contact info for attorneys, CPAs, and insurance reps
- A one-page letter explaining their values and vision for the family

They even recorded a short video explaining it all—just in case.

Credit as a Shield

Their oldest rental property was in a rougher part of town. It brought in steady income, but also came with occasional drama—plumbing issues, noise complaints, a former tenant who had threatened to sue over "unsafe stairs."

That was when Elijah decided to restructure the property into its own **LLC** and purchase an **umbrella insurance policy** for extra liability protection.

The costs:

- LLC filing: $160
- Annual registered agent service: $99
- Insurance premium: $384/year

He charged it all to a **business cashback card**, set to auto-pay from the property's rent income.

"Credit isn't just for growth," he told Ari later. "It's also for defense."

The Breakthrough Moment

Weeks later, Elijah and Camila sat down for a review with their CPA. She was impressed.

"You two have a real structure now," she said. "A legacy plan."

She offered to help them set up **529 college savings plans** for the kids—using rental income or excess credit limits from business rewards cards to pre-fund tax-advantaged education accounts.

They agreed.

Even Micah, who hated math, leaned into the idea. "You mean... you're using credit cards to save for college?"

Elijah grinned. "The smart way. You'll learn."

More Than Money

One evening, Camila caught Ari rewatching the video they had recorded for the family legacy book.

"What are you doing?" she asked, surprised.

"I don't know," Ari shrugged. "It's just cool. You and Dad... built all this. Not just the houses. The plan."

Camila smiled.

That was the moment she knew this wasn't just about credit, or money, or paperwork.

It was about **intentionality**.

About **breaking cycles**.

About handing the next generation more than just keys and passwords—handing them the tools and wisdom to grow what was already planted.

Chapter 7: Teaching Children and Teens to Build Credit Early and Responsibly

Building wealth isn't just about you–it's about empowering your children with the skills, habits, and tools to make smart financial decisions. The earlier they learn how credit works, the sooner they can begin building a strong credit profile, avoid common mistakes, and create their own path to financial independence.

This chapter will guide you in teaching your children about credit in **practical, age-appropriate ways**, and show you how to help them **build real credit** before they turn 18—or right after.

Why Teaching Credit Early Changes Generations

Most young adults don't learn about credit until they're denied for an apartment, car loan, or credit card. By then, they're playing catch-up.

Teaching kids about credit while they're still under your roof can help them:

- Avoid debt traps and credit card misuse
- Qualify for better loans when they're ready to buy a car

or home

- Build a foundation of financial responsibility
- Learn to use leverage wisely, not emotionally

By the time they're 21, they could have a **750+ credit score** and access to funding for their first business, education, or investment opportunity—**without needing a co-signer**.

Age-Appropriate Credit Lessons for Kids and Teens

You don't need a textbook. You need conversations and hands-on experiences.

Ages 6–10: Early Awareness

- Teach the difference between "buy now" and "pay later"
- Use a toy or game-based allowance system to show how earning and saving works
- Explain what a debit card is and how it's connected to real money

Ages 11–13: Introduction to Credit

- Introduce the idea of borrowing vs. owning

- Use a mock credit score game (ex: earn points for completing chores on time)
- Talk about good vs. bad uses of borrowing (investing vs. impulse buying)

Ages 14–17: Simulated Credit Experience

- Open a **youth checking account with a debit card**
- Use budgeting apps like Greenlight or Step that show spending habits
- Give them a prepaid card and let them "manage" their own monthly mini-budget
- Assign them to track a household bill (electricity, groceries, etc.) to understand budgeting

Helping Your Teen Build Real Credit Before Age 18

Yes—your teenager can begin building a real credit profile **with your help**.

Option 1: Add Them as an Authorized User

- Add them to a **seasoned credit card account** that:
    - Has been open for 2+ years

  - Has perfect payment history
  - Keeps utilization under 10%

- Most major card issuers report authorized user history to the credit bureaus

Within 60–90 days, your teen could have a FICO score of 700+ with no debt.

Option 2: Open a Secured Card in Their Name (18+)

- Once they turn 18, help them open a **secured credit card** with a $300–$500 deposit
- Teach them to use it only for small, predictable purchases (gas, groceries)
- Set up automatic payments to prevent late fees

Create a Family Credit Curriculum

Create a weekly or monthly "Money Talk" where your family sits down for 20–30 minutes to cover:

- What credit scores mean
- Why interest rates matter
- How to read a credit report

- How to use credit cards responsibly
- Real-life consequences of poor credit decisions

Bonus Project:

Assign your teen to research 3 credit cards, compare fees, APRs, and rewards—and present which one they would choose and why. Treat it like a credit "science fair."

Empower Their Credit Journey With a Purpose

The goal isn't just to give your teen access to credit—it's to give them a reason to use it responsibly. Help them:

- Set a goal: "Build 750 credit score by 21 to buy first car/home without a co-signer."
- Tie credit to opportunity: "Use my strong credit to get a business credit card and start my own online shop."
- Show the timeline: "Every payment builds your future. Every mistake sets it back."

Encourage them to track their credit with tools like:

- Credit Karma (free, educational)
- MyFICO (accurate for planning major purchases)

- Experian Boost (report utility bills for a score lift)

Chapter Summary:

- Teaching your kids about credit early prevents future mistakes and empowers them to succeed independently.
- Use age-appropriate tools and conversations to make credit a part of normal family life.
- Help them build actual credit with authorized user accounts or secured cards.
- Connect credit to real goals—college, car, business, or real estate—to make it meaningful.

"The Teen With a 740"

Marcus stood nervously in front of his high school's entrepreneurship club, holding a whiteboard with numbers scribbled in blue marker. "This month," he said, voice steady, "our sticker business cleared $1,204 in profit. We're reinvesting $400 into new designs and the rest... well, we're saving it to launch our Shopify store."

Applause broke out. One student raised a hand.

"How old are you again?"

"Sixteen."

A Different Kind of Talk

Marcus wasn't a typical teenager. He wasn't obsessed with shoes, gaming, or TikTok dances. He was obsessed with **credit**.

It all started when his dad, Jordan, handed him a printed credit score chart at the dinner table one evening.

"You can either learn about this now," Jordan said, "or wait until a bank denies you for something important later."

Marcus was confused. Credit? Wasn't that for grown-ups?

But Jordan explained: "How you use credit is how you build your future. We didn't grow up with this knowledge. You will."

The Authorized User Hack

That night, Jordan pulled up his credit card dashboard and added Marcus as an **authorized user** to his oldest card—15 years old, perfect payment history, and a low balance.

Within a few weeks, Marcus had a real credit file and a FICO score of 740.

He didn't even have a job yet. But he had a **track record**.

With that boost, they applied for a **student credit card** under Marcus's name, co-signed by Jordan. It had a $500 limit.

Marcus was instructed to only use it for:

- Gas
- School supplies
- One monthly streaming subscription

Each Sunday, they reviewed the charges. Marcus paid it off from his part-time tutoring gig.

By month three, his credit utilization was under 10%, and his payment history was perfect.

The Sticker Business

During summer break, Marcus came up with an idea: a custom motivational sticker brand for students and young athletes.

He used **$300 from his credit card** to buy a Cricut cutting machine and sticker paper. Jordan helped him register a **small LLC** for $150.

They built a simple Shopify site. His mom, Tanya, a part-time graphic designer, helped create the first sticker pack: "Grind Now, Chill Later."

Sales came in through TikTok and word of mouth at school.

The profits? Reinvested into bulk materials and shipping supplies—all managed through a **business debit card** tied to their LLC bank account.

Marcus handled:

- Order fulfillment
- Customer emails
- TikTok content

Jordan tracked the business credit file using NAV and added a Quill and Uline account to start building vendor credit under Marcus's new company.

Financial Confidence at 16

Marcus had a routine.

- Mondays: fulfill sticker orders
- Wednesdays: record new TikToks

- Sundays: review credit usage, spending, and income with his parents

He had:

- A 740 credit score
- A profitable side business
- A checking, savings, and business account
- A basic understanding of credit lines, APRs, and vendor accounts

But most importantly, he had **confidence**.

Confidence to say "no" when friends tried to convince him to max his card on designer shoes. Confidence to pitch his sticker packs to a local school supply store. Confidence to explain interest rates to a teacher who still used payday loans.

Looking Ahead

By 18, Marcus planned to:

- Apply for his first high-limit student business credit card
- Lease office space (a small garage) using business credit

- Expand into apparel
- Create an affiliate program for other teen entrepreneurs

His parents watched with quiet pride.

“We didn’t have this kind of start,” Jordan said. “But now our son does.”

Marcus smiled when people called him “disciplined” or “business-minded.” He knew the truth: He just had **access**, **education**, and a head start most teens never get.

And it all started with a dinner table talk about a credit score chart.

Chapter 8: Using Credit to Build or Buy Family-Owned Businesses

Owning a family business is one of the most powerful ways to generate wealth across generations. Whether you're **starting a new business from scratch** or **buying an existing one**, credit can give you the capital needed to launch, grow, or acquire income-generating operations—without waiting years to save.

This chapter will show you how to use personal and business credit to **start or purchase profitable family-owned businesses** and turn them into long-term assets that create income, employment, and legacy.

Why Family-Owned Businesses Create Lasting Wealth

When you own a business—especially one that involves your family—you're doing more than just making money:

- You're **controlling your income**
- You're **teaching your children entrepreneurial skills**
- You're building something that can be **passed down or sold**

- You're opening doors to tax advantages, funding, and flexibility

Unlike a job, which ends when you stop working, a business can pay you even while you sleep—or when your children take over.

Choosing the Right Business for Your Family

Your business doesn't have to be big—it just needs to be **scalable, manageable, and profitable**.

Start-from-scratch business ideas:

- **Mobile car wash/detailing**
- **Online store for handmade products**
- **Tutoring, coaching, or online courses**
- **Cleaning services (home or commercial)**
- **Airbnb or short-term rental management**
- **Lawn care and outdoor services**
- **Vending machine or ATM routes**

Buy-an-existing-business ideas:

- **Cash-flowing eCommerce websites**
- **Service businesses on Flippa, BizBuySell, or Empire Flippers**
- **Brick-and-mortar businesses with retiring owners**
- **Digital assets (courses, blogs, affiliate sites)**

Tip: Look for businesses with **recurring revenue**, **low overhead**, and **clear growth potential.**

Using Credit to Start a Family Business

Once you've chosen the right business model, credit can help you move fast and with minimal risk.

Funding sources:

1. **0% APR Business Credit Cards**
    - Fund inventory, equipment, or marketing.
    - Many offer 12–18 months of interest-free financing.
    - Examples: Chase Ink Business, Amex Blue Business, Capital One Spark.

2. **Business Lines of Credit**

    - Revolving access to capital as needed.
    - Useful for hiring, expansion, or purchasing recurring supplies.

3. **Personal Credit Cards (carefully)**

    - Best used for startup services: design, legal filing, web hosting.
    - Avoid carrying long-term balances here; pay off quickly.

4. **Vendor Credit Accounts (Net 30)**

    - Build business credit by ordering and paying vendors on time.
    - Helps you qualify for larger credit lines later.

Example: Start a vending business using a $5,000 credit card to buy machines and products. Break even in 3–6 months. Profit for years.

Buying an Existing Business Using Credit

If you prefer to skip the startup phase, you can buy a business that's already running—using a mix of credit and negotiation.

How to do it:

1. **Find the Right Business**
   - Search Flippa, Empire Flippers, or local listings.
   - Look for 2–3 years of profit history, low churn, and consistent customers.
2. **Use Business Credit for Purchase**
   - Some businesses under $25K can be purchased outright with credit cards or business credit lines.
   - Negotiate seller financing—many owners will accept 30–50% down, with the rest paid over time.
   - Use credit to fund the down payment or cover legal/accounting due diligence.
3. **Leverage the Business's Own Cash Flow**
   - Ideally, the business you buy should help you pay back the credit used to buy it.
   - Make sure the business covers its own debt within 12–18 months.

Involve Your Family in the Business

Once the business is launched or acquired, bring the family in.

Roles could include:

- **Spouse**: Accounting, marketing, customer service
- **Teenagers**: Tech, design, video, social media
- **Children**: Product assembly, labeling, cleaning, basic admin tasks
- **Parents/Relatives**: Delivery, bookkeeping, mentorship, vendor calls

This helps reduce hiring costs, build teamwork, and **teach real financial skills** in the home.

> Bonus: Children working in the business may qualify for **tax-free income up to $14,000/year**, depending on your entity structure.

Protect and Scale the Business with Credit

After the business is running:

- Use credit for **bulk inventory** or supplier negotiations

- Apply for a **business credit line** to cover seasonal dips
- Use **credit to invest in automation**, such as software, CRM tools, and email marketing
- Get an **LLC, insurance, and emergency credit fund** for legal and financial protection

Always keep **credit separate** from personal life to avoid overleveraging.

Pro tip: Create a separate "growth fund" credit card used only for things that generate ROI: ads, new equipment, or bulk inventory buys with discounts.

Chapter Summary:

- Family businesses build income, skills, and legacy—and credit makes starting or buying one faster and easier.
- Use credit strategically for startup or acquisition—not lifestyle expenses.
- Choose simple, scalable business models and involve your family in daily operations.
- Reinvest profits, build credit lines, and protect your business like an asset.

- Treat the business as a long-term tool for freedom—not just income.

"The Digital Rescue"

The Gutierrez family never planned on buying a business.

Luis worked as a warehouse supervisor. His wife, Daniela, ran a small Etsy shop selling handmade jewelry. Their teenage son, Nico, was a tech-savvy high schooler with dreams of starting a YouTube channel. They were a tight-knit family living in Central Texas—practical, humble, and cautious with money.

But in the spring of that year, everything changed.

The Fork in the Road

Luis's company announced layoffs.

He wasn't laid off—yet. But the writing was on the wall. Schedules were cut, overtime disappeared, and Luis was told to "start preparing for change."

That night at dinner, Daniela spoke first.

"What if this is our push?"

Luis looked up. "Push for what?"

"To finally own something. Something we control. Something that doesn't depend on someone else's schedule."

Luis shook his head. "We don't have the cash to open a store."

Daniela slid her laptop across the table. "We don't need one."

On the screen was a listing on Flippa.com: **"Profitable Children's Activity Blog with Passive Income – $9,800 OBO."**

A Family Business Online

The blog was run by a stay-at-home mom who was shifting careers. It had 200+ articles, 5 years of traffic history, email subscribers, and affiliate revenue from Amazon.

It was making **$400–$600/month**—consistently.

Daniela loved the niche. Luis was intrigued by the income. Nico? He immediately started brainstorming video content for a connected YouTube channel.

"We can buy this," Daniela said, "and make it ours."

They applied for a **business credit card** that came with 0% interest for 12 months. Luis had solid credit and was approved for a $15,000 limit.

They used **$9,800** to buy the blog. They spent another **$1,200** on legal review and transferring hosting. And they set aside **$500** for redesigning the site and buying content tools like Canva Pro, Jasper AI, and ConvertKit.

Total cost: **$11,500**, all on the card.

Monthly payment (at 0%): **$958**, which they planned to pay off using the blog's cash flow and Daniela's Etsy profits.

Making It a Family Operation

In the first 60 days, they:

- Rebranded the blog as *LittleExplorersClub.com*
- Added Daniela's printable craft guides from Etsy to boost affiliate earnings
- Started collecting emails and built an 800-subscriber list
- Connected Nico's new YouTube channel to the blog with simple how-to craft videos

Luis handled logistics and affiliate accounts. Daniela wrote blog content and newsletters. Nico handled SEO, thumbnails, and video edits—something he enjoyed more than homework.

They didn't have employees. They didn't even have office space. Just a corner desk, a free email platform, and a shared family calendar.

But they had something better: **ownership**.

The Tipping Point

By month five, traffic had grown 40% thanks to new blog posts and Pinterest promotion.

Their monthly revenue hit $980—just enough to cover the business card payment.

By month seven, they landed a small sponsorship from a toy brand.

By month nine, Nico's videos had passed 10,000 views, and the YouTube channel was monetized.

Luis was still at the warehouse—barely.

When the layoff finally came, he wasn't scared.

He was ready.

The Reinvention

Luis took a severance check and immediately paid off the remaining card balance—just over $2,000. Their credit score had gone up, not down, because of low utilization and on-time payments.

They reinvested into:

- A virtual assistant to manage Pinterest and email
- New video equipment for Nico
- An online course teaching how to start a craft blog (their own digital product)

The blog became a **business.** The business became an **asset.** The asset became a **family-owned income stream.**

By the one-year mark, they were earning over **$2,700/month** in a combination of:

- Affiliate income
- YouTube ads
- Sponsored content
- Their digital course
- Printable sales

They were no longer just reacting to layoffs and economic swings.

They were running their own economy.

Beyond the Business

At a family BBQ, Nico's uncle asked him, "What do you want to do after high school?"

Nico shrugged. "I'm already doing it."

Daniela smiled. "We built this together."

Luis added, "And credit made it possible—not because we spent wildly, but because we used it like a tool."

The Gutierrez family didn't buy a store. They didn't build a restaurant. They didn't open a franchise.

They bought a quiet little blog—and turned it into a business that made more than any job had ever offered them.

And now, they were ready to buy another.

Chapter 9: Automating and Delegating with Credit to Free Up Family Time

One of the greatest benefits of building family wealth through credit is the ability to **buy back your time**. As your income streams grow, you'll eventually hit a point where your most limited resource isn't money—it's time.

This chapter teaches you how to use personal and business credit to **automate, outsource, and delegate** the repetitive parts of your income streams or household management. The result? More freedom, less burnout, and a business that runs even when you're not working.

The Problem with Doing Everything Yourself

At the beginning of your journey, it's normal to wear multiple hats—entrepreneur, bookkeeper, marketer, tech support. But if you don't start automating or delegating, you'll quickly hit a wall:

- You'll become the bottleneck of your own business.
- Growth will stall because you can't scale yourself.
- Your family life will suffer as work consumes every free moment.

The solution isn't working harder. It's working **smarter**—with help from **systems, software, and strategic spending**.

What to Automate First Using Credit

Here are the **best tasks to automate first**, using affordable software or one-time purchases—funded with 0% APR cards or business credit:

Income Stream Automations:

- **Email marketing:** Use ConvertKit, Mailchimp, or Systeme.io to automate welcome emails, promotions, and abandoned cart recovery.
- **Online sales:** Shopify or Etsy integration to auto-fulfill digital products or notify for physical shipments.
- **Payments & invoicing:** Use Stripe, PayPal, or Square for recurring billing and client management.
- **Appointment booking:** Use Calendly or Acuity for service-based businesses.

Household & Admin Automations:

- **Bill pay:** Automate recurring bills and credit payments to avoid late fees.

- **Budget tracking:** Use Mint, YNAB, or Rocket Money to monitor finances.
- **Grocery delivery subscriptions:** Use Instacart, Amazon Fresh, or Walmart+ to save time.
- **Subscription management:** Use Truebill to track and cancel wasteful recurring charges.

Tip: Many of these platforms offer annual payment discounts—use a business credit card to lock in the savings upfront.

Strategic Delegation Using Credit

Once you've automated the basics, it's time to **outsource tasks** that don't require your direct involvement. This doesn't mean hiring full-time employees. You can start small:

Delegation Options:

1. **Freelancers on Fiverr or Upwork:**
    - Graphic design, video editing, email sequences, blog writing.
    - Use business credit to prepay for project packages.

2. **Virtual Assistants (VAs):**
   - Hire VAs from the Philippines, Latin America, or Eastern Europe for $4–$10/hour.
   - Use VAs for customer service, inbox management, content repurposing, and more.
3. **Local Help:**
   - Teens can pack orders or manage social media.
   - Family members can be paid tax-deductible wages through your business.

   Consider paying monthly VA or freelancer contracts via credit cards to **earn points** while covering business expenses—just don't carry balances long-term.

Calculate the ROI of Buying Back Time

If you're hesitant to spend, use this formula:

What's your hourly value? Let's say you make $3,000/month from your online store. You work 60 hours. That's **$50/hour**.

If you spend 8 hours a week editing videos yourself (instead of working on strategy or sales), that's **$400/week** in lost opportunity.

Hiring a freelancer for $100/week returns $300 in time value to you.

Using credit to frontload that expense while the income continues flowing is not wasteful—it's **smart leverage**.

Automate and Delegate Without Losing Control

Automating and outsourcing doesn't mean disappearing. Stay involved by:

- Using project management tools like Trello, Notion, or ClickUp to manage freelancers.
- Holding a 30-minute weekly "business team" check-in with your spouse, VA, or kids.
- Reviewing income and expenses once a week to stay ahead of spending.

Use credit-backed services that allow **pause, control, and metrics**, like:

- Ad platforms with set spend caps
- Email tools with detailed open/click reports

- VA time-tracking software like Time Doctor

How Families Can Use Credit to Buy Time Together

The ultimate goal of building credit-funded income streams is **time freedom**. Use your improved credit to:

- Prepay for vacations using travel cards with cashback
- Invest in time-saving services like cleaning, laundry, or tutoring
- Buy devices and software that reduce repetitive work
- Use rewards to book flights, hotels, or meals as a family

Example: Use a travel rewards business card to fund your ecommerce growth. The points can cover family travel later—giving both income and memories.

Chapter Summary:

- Automate the repetitive tasks in your business and household to free up your time.
- Use credit to front-load time-saving software and outsource help without draining cash.
- Track ROI: spend $1 on automation or help that gives

you $3–$5 in time or income back.

- Don't delegate everything—delegate strategically and stay involved.
- Use time freedom to invest in your family, health, and long-term goals.

"Time Bought Back"

The Patel family had a problem that didn't look like a problem to most people.

Business was booming.

Their digital planner shop on Etsy had crossed $7,000 in monthly revenue. Their YouTube channel—run by their 16-year-old daughter, Aanya—had just passed 25,000 subscribers. They had three online courses, a dozen printable products, and a growing customer base.

But they were exhausted.

The Breaking Point

It was a Saturday afternoon when Priya Patel finally snapped.

She sat at the dining table, buried in customer emails, watching cold tea sweat into a napkin. Her husband, Raj, had been troubleshooting the checkout page on their website for over an hour. Their kids were arguing about chores, and laundry sat untouched in a hallway basket.

This wasn't the freedom they envisioned when they started their business.

"We created this to get more time," Priya said, frustrated. "And now we have less of it than ever."

Raj sighed, rubbing his forehead. "We either shut half of this down... or we figure out how to run it **without** running ourselves into the ground."

The Automation Plan

That night, Raj reviewed their credit account. They had a **$12,000 business credit card** with 0% interest for 10 months.

They didn't want to use it to buy more stuff. They wanted to buy **time.**

So, they made a plan.

Phase 1: Automation

- Moved their courses from a clunky WordPress site to **Kajabi** (paid annually to save 20%)

- Switched email marketing to **ConvertKit**, automating all welcome emails, abandoned cart sequences, and weekly broadcasts

- Set up **Zapier** to connect customer actions across platforms (ex: new order triggers a review request + upsell email)

- Used **Canva Pro** to create and auto-schedule Pinterest and Instagram posts

All expenses? Charged to the business credit card—paid back monthly from business profits.

Total automation spend: **$2,400** Resulting time saved per week: **15 hours**

The Delegation Shift

With the basics automated, Priya tackled customer support—her biggest time drain.

They hired a **virtual assistant** from the Philippines for $6/hour, 20 hours/week. She handled:

- Etsy messages

- Refund requests

- Upload errors
- Positive review follow-ups

Next, they hired a **Fiverr freelancer** to redesign outdated thumbnails for their digital products and course pages.

Aanya, their daughter, took over weekly YouTube editing using **CapCut**, which they paid $75/year for via credit.

Delegation spend:

- VA: $480/month
- Fiverr: $300 one-time
- Software: $75/year

They tracked every ROI in a simple Google Sheet.

The Results

Within three months, they:

- Reduced weekly work hours from 50+ to 15–20
- Increased monthly sales by 18% (thanks to improved systems and follow-ups)

- Brought customer support response time from 48 hours to under 6
- Took their first **3-day weekend trip** in over a year—paid entirely with **credit card reward points**

Priya no longer felt chained to her inbox. Raj wasn't fixing broken links at midnight. Aanya was proud of being part of a real business—and finally had time for SAT prep.

And surprisingly, their **profit** didn't drop.

It grew.

Buying Back Their Life

With systems in place, they used the freed-up time to:

- Plan a second digital product line (student planners)
- Launch a podcast using their existing email list
- Start a weekend cooking class in their community—just for fun

But more than that, they got their **life** back.

They cooked together again. Took long walks. Played board games without someone checking Shopify notifications every ten minutes.

Their business didn't stop working when they stopped.

It ran **because they stopped micromanaging.**

A Family in Control

At their family meeting, Priya laid out their new weekly roles:

- Raj would monitor analytics and ads
- Aanya would handle creative tasks and YouTube
- The VA and freelancers would handle routine work
- Priya would oversee product development and partnerships

"This," Raj said, looking around the room, "is why we did all of this. To live, not just earn."

They had built a business that worked for them—not the other way around.

And they did it using credit **not to consume**, but to **free themselves**.

Time, they learned, is the most valuable currency.

And thanks to smart planning, they finally had enough of it.

Chapter 10: Scaling Wealth Through Credit-Funded Real Estate and Business Expansion

You've laid the foundation: credit is strong, income streams are flowing, and your family understands how to manage money and leverage wisely. Now it's time for the next step—**scaling**.

In this chapter, we'll cover how to use personal and business credit to **expand your wealth portfolio**, scale what's already working, and move from "extra income" to **true generational wealth** through **credit-powered growth**.

What Scaling Really Means

Scaling isn't just doing more—it's about:

- Multiplying income without multiplying effort
- Expanding successful models instead of starting over
- Using **credit, systems, and people** to increase profit and ownership

Whether you're growing your real estate portfolio or expanding your online business, the goal is the same: **use**

other people's money (credit) to build more **assets**, not liabilities.

Scaling a Real Estate Portfolio with Credit

If you've acquired one rental, Airbnb, or BRRRR property using credit, scaling is simply a matter of **repeating the process—strategically.**

3 Ways to Scale Real Estate with Credit:

1. **Use HELOCs or Cash-Out Refinance**
    - Tap into equity from one property to fund down payments for others.
    - HELOCs can be interest-only and used flexibly.
    - Use the credit temporarily, then refinance after appreciation.
2. **Business Credit for Renovations**
    - Use high-limit business cards or lines of credit to cover:
        - Appliance purchases
        - Contractor payments

        - Airbnb furnishings

    - Pay them down with cash flow or refinance proceeds.

3. **Partner with Family Using Credit**

    - Bring in relatives as co-borrowers or investors.
    - Pool personal and business credit capacity.
    - Set up an LLC with shared roles and profits.

   Example: You buy one Airbnb using $15K from a HELOC. After a year of positive cash flow, use those profits and equity growth to purchase another—and repeat.

Scaling a Business With Credit-Funded Expansion

Your business doesn't have to be big to grow. Start with what's working, then pour fuel (credit) on it.

Methods to Scale a Business:

1. **Inventory Expansion**

    - Use 0% cards or vendor credit to buy inventory in bulk at discounts.

- Improves profit margins and speeds up order fulfillment.

2. **Advertising & Marketing**
    - Scale ad campaigns that already convert.
    - Fund paid ads on YouTube, Facebook, or Google using business cards.
    - Track ROI with tools like Hyros or Meta Ad Manager.
3. **New Product Lines or Services**
    - Use credit to test new offers without dipping into savings.
    - Launch a second digital course, product, or membership using previous profits and credit.
4. **System Upgrades**
    - Pay for CRM systems (like GoHighLevel, Kartra, or Kajabi) to automate sales pipelines.
    - Use credit to hire or upgrade fulfillment, bookkeeping, or virtual teams.

Tip: Apply for **multiple credit lines in a 2-week window** to minimize credit inquiries' impact and stack available capital.

Managing Credit and Risk as You Scale

Scaling increases opportunity—but also risk. Protect your growing business or real estate portfolio by:

- Keeping **utilization under 30%** to avoid score drops
- Setting up **LLCs for each property or brand** to isolate liability
- Building a **cash buffer** alongside credit expansion
- Using business insurance, umbrella policies, and contracts with clear terms
- Monitoring credit reports monthly (NAV for business, Credit Karma for personal)

Create a **credit dashboard** to track:

- Available limits
- Current balances
- Interest-free periods

- Payment dates

Use this dashboard to rotate credit usage, prevent overexposure, and preserve your ability to borrow again when needed.

Know When to Transition From Credit to Capital

Eventually, the goal is to shift from **credit-funded** to **cash-flow funded** growth.

Here's when to consider transitioning:

- Your business consistently generates $10K+/month
- You've built up 3–6 months of reserves
- Your assets can qualify for traditional lending (like SBA loans or commercial financing)
- You want to reduce exposure and improve debt-to-income ratios

At that point, you can use credit **strategically**, not out of necessity.

Scaling as a Family Mission

Scaling works best when it becomes a family mission—not just your solo hustle.

- Assign clear roles in real estate, ecommerce, or content creation
- Involve teens in outreach, marketing, or research
- Share the wins—track new income milestones together
- Celebrate with experiences, not just purchases
- Set new family goals each quarter: "Acquire one new asset," "Launch one new product," or "Pay off one funding source"

Scaling becomes legacy when it becomes **shared ownership**.

Chapter Summary:

- Scaling wealth is about multiplying what works—without increasing your stress.
- Use credit to expand real estate, inventory, ad spend, and automation.
- Protect your gains with legal entities, insurance, and proper risk management.
- Transition from credit to cash-flow-funded growth over time.

- Make wealth-building a family-centered, mission-driven process.

"The $250K Family Empire"

The Flores family didn't look like entrepreneurs.

Carla was a former dental assistant who started selling printable chore charts on Etsy to keep busy after being laid off. Her husband, Mateo, was a part-time landscaper who worked with his father's company. They lived in a modest home in Bakersfield, California, with their three kids—Luca (14), Mia (11), and baby Sofia.

Their first digital product sale brought in $6.74. Carla cried.

Not because it was a lot of money—but because it proved something they had started together could **work**.

They didn't know it yet, but that little Etsy sale would become the first spark of a **$250,000/year family business**—fueled by **credit**, teamwork, and a relentless commitment to growth.

From Kitchen Table to Online Shop

The first year was humble.

Carla made chore charts, homeschool printables, and teacher rewards for parents and educators. She learned how to bundle products, optimize keywords, and design in Canva. Mateo supported from the sidelines, picking up groceries, watching Sofia during nap time, and helping ship any physical versions they offered locally.

They used a **$3,500 personal credit card** to buy:

- Canva Pro and Creative Fabrica for assets
- An Epson EcoTank printer for test prints
- Their first Etsy ads campaign

Within 6 months, the shop was making $2,000/month.

They paid off the card in full—and **raised their credit limit**.

The First Scaling Decision

Late one night, after the kids had gone to sleep, Mateo asked a simple question: "What would happen if we really went for it?"

Carla paused. "You mean... like full time?"

They had $4,200 in savings. No safety net. But they had momentum.

They applied for a **business credit card** using Carla's growing income and were approved for **$9,000 at 0% APR for 12 months.**

They used it to:

- Hire a Fiverr designer to refresh their store branding
- Launch a Shopify site to sell directly
- Invest in bulk inventory for their new printable planners + bonus inserts
- Subscribe to **email marketing software** and start building a list

Mateo took a step back from landscaping. Mia and Luca helped organize orders and test new product ideas.

Family Business in Full Swing

By year two, their daily routine looked like this:

- **Carla**: Product creation, SEO, marketing
- **Mateo**: Shopify operations, supplier management, shipping
- **Luca**: YouTube tutorials on how to use printables (growing the channel to 15K subs)

- **Mia**: Product tester and TikTok clips with short tips and home hacks
- **Sofia**: Napping (most days)

They hired a **virtual assistant** for $350/month to:

- Handle customer service
- Send follow-up emails
- Monitor Etsy messages and reviews

They used credit to prepay the VA's contract for 6 months—saving $300 and earning cashback.

Real Estate Dreams & Scaling Up

With business profits reaching **$12,000/month**, they started looking at short-term rentals.

Mateo applied for a **home equity line of credit** (HELOC) on their primary residence—now worth $80,000 more than when they bought it.

They pulled **$50,000** from the HELOC and used it as a down payment on a **2-bedroom condo** in Big Bear, California, just a few hours from home. They furnished it with cashback points from their business card.

They automated the Airbnb listing, hired local cleaners, and set up remote check-in.

First month? Fully booked. Net profit: **$1,100** after expenses.

They now had two engines:

1. A growing digital products business
2. A credit-funded rental property

Managing Growth With a Plan

With systems in place, they built a credit strategy dashboard in Google Sheets. They tracked:

- Available limits
- Usage per card
- Due dates and grace periods
- Business ROI per expense

They rotated between 3 cards:

- One for **ads and marketing**
- One for **inventory and tools**
- One for **travel and rewards**

They never paid late. Never went over 30% utilization. And every dollar spent had a clear path to income.

Mateo handled the real estate side. Carla oversaw product launches and email sequences. The kids? They now had debit cards, budgeting apps, and biweekly "business review" meetings.

The Legacy in Motion

In year three, the Flores family business passed **$250,000 in annual revenue**.

They had:

- Over 400 products on Etsy and Shopify
- A monetized YouTube channel
- Two short-term rental properties
- Three high-limit business credit cards
- A growing list of over 12,000 email subscribers
- A written family financial blueprint

Carla no longer saw herself as a "mom who got lucky." She was a **CEO, creator, and investor.**

Mateo no longer saw his value as just physical labor. He had become a financial strategist and operations leader.

They hadn't just made money.

They made a **system**. A **structure**. A **legacy**.

And they did it by leveraging credit to create not debt—but **ownership**.

The best part?

They did it **together.**

Final Words from the Author: "The Wealth Is Already in Your Hands"

When I started this book, I didn't just want to write a guide—I wanted to create a mirror.

A mirror for the parent who lies awake at night wondering if they're doing enough. A mirror for the couple who works hard but never seems to get ahead. A mirror for the young adult afraid to start because they feel behind. And most of all, a mirror for the families—just like yours—who have more potential than they've ever been told.

Because the truth is this:

Wealth is not about being born into money. It's about being born into mindset.

And the mindset you choose—starting now—can change everything.

You Were Never Meant to Trade Time for Every Dollar

The system told you that to make money, you had to sacrifice time, energy, and presence.

You were taught to:

- Work harder, not smarter
- Save slowly instead of invest wisely
- Borrow only in desperation—not for growth
- Wait until you "have money" to start building wealth

But families who win—who build lasting wealth—**break those rules**.

They learn to:

- **Leverage credit to start income streams**
- **Automate and delegate to reclaim time**
- **Teach their children early** instead of shielding them from financial truths
- **Use structure to build legacy**, not just hustle to pay bills

And now that knowledge is in your hands.

What You've Built Throughout This Book

You haven't just read a book. You've built a toolkit.

Let's recap what you've done so far:

- Reframed credit as a tool, not a trap
- Rebuilt or optimized your personal credit file
- Learned to build business credit and use it to fund new ventures
- Started or acquired a family business or property
- Created multiple income streams that don't rely on a paycheck
- Protected your family's wealth with insurance, trusts, and LLCs
- Taught your children how credit works
- Automated your life so that you can **live**, not just earn
- Scaled with intention—not chaos
- Built a roadmap to make sure the wealth continues long after you're gone

You've gone from borrower to **builder**. From employee to **entrepreneur**. From worried parent to **family leader**.

That's no small journey.

If You're Feeling Overwhelmed, That's Okay

You don't have to do everything at once.

Some families start with fixing credit. Others launch a digital product. Some go straight into real estate or buying a business.

There is no "perfect order." There is only **consistent action.**

One smart move per week. One bill automated. One credit line secured. One conversation with your kids about money. One new idea tested.

Compound that over a year, and your entire life looks different.

You don't need a six-figure income. You don't need 100,000 followers. You don't even need a college degree.

You just need what you already have:

- Discipline
- Curiosity
- A plan
- And a reason

If your reason is your family—you're already wealthier than most.

What I Wish Someone Told Me Sooner

If I could go back 20 years and hand myself a letter, it would say this:

> "Credit isn't evil. It's a shortcut—if you treat it with respect.
>
> Start the business. Buy the duplex. Get the card with points.
>
> But only swipe if you know how the swipe pays you back.
>
> Teach your kids what you weren't taught. Show them a different life.
>
> Money isn't everything—but **freedom is**, and wealth is just freedom repeated across generations.
>
> Don't wait until you're desperate. Build while things are calm.
>
> Time is your greatest asset. Buy it back early. Use it well."

I now know that every dollar I borrowed—when used correctly—was actually a **down payment on freedom.**

And the faster you believe that, the faster you change your entire trajectory.

You Are the Blueprint Now

Here's what happens next:

Your family starts to ask questions. Neighbors start noticing you don't work weekends anymore. Your kids repeat phrases you've taught them: "Is this a liability or an asset?" Your spouse doesn't worry when bills come in—they ask, "How do we grow from here?"

That's the power of transformation.

And you're not just living it—you're leading it.

You are now the example someone else is waiting for. You are now the story your children will tell. You are now the **blueprint** for someone else's breakthrough.

Own it.

The Journey Doesn't End Here

This isn't the end. This is your beginning.

My challenge to you is simple:

- Choose the **first credit move** you'll make this week—big or small.
- Write out your **3-month family wealth goal**—and share it with someone.
- Schedule your **first (or next) family money talk**—even if it's just 15 minutes.
- And start tracking your progress like a real business—because your family is one.

If this book helped you, **pay it forward**.

Share it with a friend, a cousin, or a neighbor who's still stuck in survival mode. Show them the page that lit something up in you. Because there's enough for all of us to win.

The Quiet Revolution Happening in Homes Like Yours

There's a quiet revolution happening—not on Wall Street, not in Silicon Valley, and not in million-dollar boardrooms.

It's happening in **living rooms**, **kitchen tables**, and **home offices** all across the country.

Parents are learning what schools never taught them. Teenagers are launching businesses from laptops. Families are flipping the script—trading fear for financial literacy, debt for leverage, and survival for **ownership**.

And if you've made it this far in the book, you're part of it.

A New Type of Wealth Builder

Wealth used to look a certain way.

Suits. Stocks. Fancy terms. Old money.

But that's changing.

Today's wealth builder:

- Shops at Costco
- Uses reward points to buy groceries

- Builds LLCs on weekends
- Has a family bank account and a side hustle
- Reads their kid bedtime stories and teaches them about passive income
- Fixes credit, not to flash a lifestyle, but to **build freedom**

You are the new face of generational wealth. You are the new normal.

And you didn't wait for permission—you started.

What the Data Can't Measure

The statistics won't show the real transformation.

They won't show:

- The pride in a mother's eyes when she teaches her daughter how a credit score works
- The relief on a father's face when his side hustle covers the mortgage
- The giggles of a teenager opening their first debit card and logging a sale

- The notebook filled with credit card payment plans and business ideas
- The couple who argued about money last year now strategizing together every Sunday

These are the moments that redefine families—not just financially, but emotionally.

Wealth isn't just a number.

It's peace.

It's time.

It's options.

It's dignity.

And it's being passed down—one household at a time.

This Is Not About Perfection

You'll make mistakes.

You might overextend one month. Miss a payment. Launch a product that flops. Partner with the wrong person. Panic during a recession. Delay the trust paperwork. Forget to log expenses.

That's okay.

This is not about being perfect. It's about being **present**, **intentional**, and **resilient**.

There is no wealth builder on earth who didn't fall, adjust, learn, and come back smarter.

Your only job is to keep going—with wisdom and with purpose.

Look How Far You've Come

Let's take a moment to acknowledge what most won't.

You showed up. You made it to the final chapter. You absorbed uncomfortable truths and exciting possibilities. You opened your mind to tools that may have once scared or confused you. You made plans for your children—plans no one made for you.

That is extraordinary.

Wealth is not measured by how many dollars you make. It's measured by how many **limits you remove**—from yourself and from your family.

And you've removed a lot.

Take a moment. Breathe. Be proud. Because what you're building isn't temporary. It's not for show. It's not based on trends.

It's real.

The Next Generation Is Watching

You may not realize it now, but your kids are listening.

They hear you when you say, "That's not in the budget." They see you when you sit down with a calculator instead of buying impulsively. They feel the difference when money isn't a source of fear—but a tool of confidence.

They're learning how to treat credit. How to treat money. How to treat their own dreams.

Every smart decision you make today becomes a shortcut for their tomorrow.

They'll borrow wiser. Build faster. Fail safer. And dream bigger.

That's the gift you've given them.

Keep the Revolution Going

This is not the end. It's a baton pass.

Now you teach. You lead. You share.

Talk to your friends. Host a dinner where you walk through your new credit system. Email your sibling and offer to help them pull their credit report. Start a blog, podcast, or family YouTube channel. Print out your financial blueprint and put it in a binder on your desk. Record a short video message to your children explaining how you built what you built.

These are not small actions.

These are **seeds**.

And when planted, they grow into family trees that bear fruit for generations—fruit of ownership, discipline, creativity, and freedom.

You've taken the first step. You've stayed the course. You've built something real.

Now go share it.

Because this isn't just your wealth.

It's your **legacy**.

Other Books in the *Credit to Capital* Series

By Joe Correa

Unlock the full financial journey with these powerful and practical books in the *Credit to Capital* series. Each volume is designed to help you build, repair, and leverage credit to create wealth, purchase property, and launch businesses—no matter where you're starting from.

- **Book 1: How to Establish Credit in the U.S.**
- **Book 2: Personal Credit Repair Blueprint**
- **Book 3: How to Build Credit Fast Without Debt**
- **Book 4: Business Credit Mastery**
- **Book 5: Credit Card Secrets for Building Wealth & Rewards**
- **Book 6: Credit Card Hacking for Smart Borrowers**
- **Book 7: How to Leverage Business Credit to Fund Real Estate Purchases**
- **Book 8: Business Credit Ecosystem: Build, Stack & Automate Unlimited Funding Without Personal Risk**
- **Book 9: How to Get $1M in Credit and Keep It**
- **Book 10: Credit-Funded Wealth for Families**

www.ingramcontent.com/pod-product-compliance
Lightning Source LLC
LaVergne TN
LVHW022226200926
848481LV00006B/2137
* 9 7 9 8 3 4 9 3 1 8 1 3 9 *